This book
belongs to:

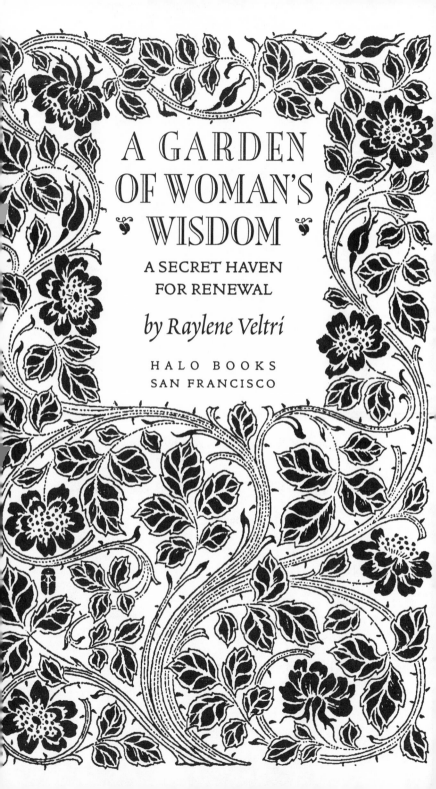

A GARDEN OF WOMAN'S WISDOM

A SECRET HAVEN FOR RENEWAL

by Raylene Veltri

HALO BOOKS
SAN FRANCISCO

Published by

HALO BOOKS
Post Office Box 2529
San Francisco, CA 94126

Printed in the United States of America

Cover and Text Design and Art Direction: Susan Larson
Typesetting and Computer Magic: Diane Spencer Hume

Library of Congress Catalog Card
Number 94-41004

Library of Congress Cataloging-in-Publication Data

Veltri, Raylene, 1951-
   A garden of woman's wisdom : a secret haven for renewal /
by Raylene Veltri.
       p.   cm. ISBN 1-879904-14-4 (pbk.) : $12.95
   1. Flowers—Quotations, maxims, etc.   2. Women—Life
skills guides.   I. Title.
PN6084.F5V44 1995
818'.5402--dc20   94-41004
                                                                CIP

The information in this book is educational, with references to health.
We do not advocate self diagnosis for anyone with continuing symp-
toms. The readers should be aware that plant substances may cause
allergic reactions in some people.

EPIGRAPH

AT the gate of the garden some stand and look within but do not care to enter. ❧ Others step inside, behold it's beauty, but do not penetrate far. ❧ Still others encircle the garden, inhale the fragrance of the flowers and pass out again by the same gate. ❧ But there are always some who enter and become intoxicated with the splendor of what they behold and remain for life to tend the garden. ❧

— by Abdul Baha

DEDICATION

*For my children Joshua, Sheenon, and Selene,
the sapphire, ruby, and emerald in my crown.
Also John, my husband, for the encouragement
he has given me along the way.*

CONTENTS

OVER the last forty years women have broken through the boundaries that for centuries have confined our minds and bodies. ❧ Contemporary women were raised by mothers who were tied to being full-time homemakers, unable to express themselves sexually or creatively without threatening society. ❧

❧ Women of the sixties became sexually liberated. In the effort to discard outdated mores, we also threw out much of what makes us women. ❧ We were in such a hurry to leave the past behind, we failed to notice the loss of our feminine virtues. ❧ Just as prison breaks leave wreckage in their wake, our newly won sexual freedom engendered a lack of responsibility that resulted in unfulfilled relationships among other things. ❧

❧ Women of the seventies were torn between workplace and birthplace. Independence produced the single parent phenomenon. We became mother and father, provider and care-giver. ❧

❧ Women of the eighties found a new threat impeding their progress: the resurgence of sexually transmitted diseases, including AIDs, caused us to be less compulsive: to rethink the nature of relationships. ❧

A NEW AGE COMETH 🌱 🌱 🌱

❧ Now we find ourselves at the dawning of a new Millennium, a time to take stock of where we've been and where we're going. ❧ Those of us with daughters of our own need to ask what kind of life and wisdom we wish to pass along to the next generation of women. ❧ My own hope is for a spiritual revolution when humankind takes one of its periodic leaps up the evolutionary ladder to a higher level of consciousness where we will no longer be burdened by useless sexist paradigms. ❧ Once lightened of that burden we can look forward to a Pax Epoch between the sexes when collectively and individually we will feel sufficiently secure to practice the Golden Rule in all our affairs. ❧

BETWIXT AND BETWEEN ❧ ❧

❧ In the meantime, however, women must deal with what is (without losing sight of what could be). ❧ For the foreseeable future we must confront challenges and manage stresses produced by the tug-of-war between the old and the new. ❧ In the nineties women are caught in the middle, half way from the past; half way into the future. ❧

RETREAT INTO NATURE 🌱 🌱

❀ The strain this daily duel places on our bodies and psyches is not to be ignored. ❀ Some relief may be found on the pages to follow. ❀ Regular walks through the Wisdom Garden can provide a much needed antidote to the rough and tumble of the unreal "real world." ❀ It is along this pathway we can find our center, along with peace, and the perspective necessary to keep our balance in the topsy-turvy world beyond the garden's gate. ❀

❀ It seems entirely appropriate that flowers would have such a benevolent affect. ❀ The garden has always been a haven. ❀ Before science and theology, plants salved our physical aches and psychic pains. ❀ The plant kingdom was woman's/man 's pharmacopoeia and altar. ❀

�֍ I have followed this path for a number of years now, and the wisdom I have gained may be summed up thus: The male and female relationship is a reflection of the inner union of God and Goddess. ❧ For what is above is also below. ❧ What is in Heaven is reflected on Earth. The separation of body from soul and sexuality from spirit can be healed as we come to understand and incorporate these truths into our daily lives. ❧

✖ The woman and female aspects have suffered through time because we have ignored our own purity and forgotten how full of grace we really are. ❧

✖ It is my hope and prayer that your life will bloom with new beauty after some time spent in the Garden of Wisdom. ❧

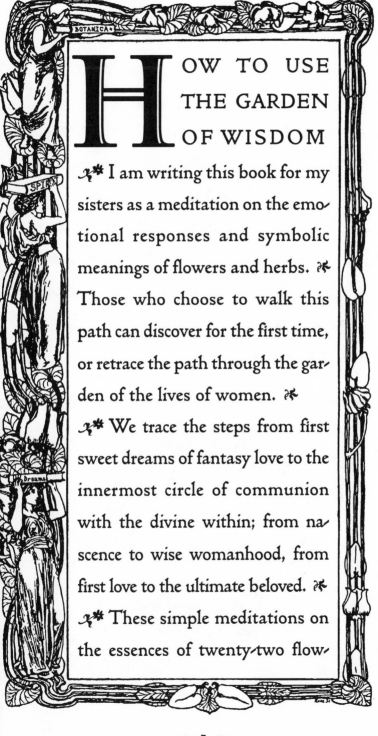

HOW TO USE THE GARDEN OF WISDOM

✗✱ I am writing this book for my sisters as a meditation on the emotional responses and symbolic meanings of flowers and herbs. ⅋✦ Those who choose to walk this path can discover for the first time, or retrace the path through the garden of the lives of women. ⅋✦

✗✱ We trace the steps from first sweet dreams of fantasy love to the innermost circle of communion with the divine within; from nascence to wise womanhood, from first love to the ultimate beloved. ⅋✦

✗✱ These simple meditations on the essences of twenty-two flowers, will help us remember our own purity as women. ❧ A liberating experience! ❧

❧ With the aid of flowers and the Garden Mandala we are invited into the realm of love and wisdom. ❧

❧ Experience each flower's message as you mindwalk the Mandala of Wisdom. ❧

❧ Pause at each flower to savor it's fragrance, remembering times you have been with this flower. ❧

THE MANDALA ITSELF IS A COMPLETE CIRCLE.

It represents wholeness, unity, and spirit. The Mandala has no beginning, no transition and no end. It is complete unto itself.

BY experiencing the different aspects of a mandala's teaching we can bring our mind, heart and spirit into a unified wholeness. ❧

❧ Great inspiration and changing of consciousness has been inspired by the mandala. ❧ Different cultures have employed the mandala for teaching: the Tibetans have beautiful paintings of the mandala showing the various aspects of gods and goddesses. ❧ Native Americans use the circle marked off in stones, known as the Medicine Wheel. ❧ The Medicine Wheel teaches different ways of being, represented by animals and the four directions. ❧ The Druids also used stone mandalas aligned with the stars and rising of the sun and the moon. ❧ Even the church of Notre Dame's famous rose window is considered a mandala, the rose representing the Blessed Mother. ❧

❧ For these reasons the Wisdom Garden is configured as a mandala. ❧ I hope it will open new pathways of wholeness and awareness to the reader. ❧

HE TWENTY-TWO FLOWERS

❧ The Native American culture says we have entered the age of flowers. ❧ This will be a time when many people will become sensitive enough to be able to gather the wisdom and the healing qualities that come from the flower kingdom. ❧ Today you see Flower Power going mainstream, from aromatherapy counters in major department stores, Bach Flower essences for emotional ills, to essential oils at your local drug store. ❧ Many people are beginning to accept the healing flowers can bring. ❧

❧ Throughout history there have been different systems which delivered the messages of flowers. ❧ The inspiration for this book came to me from the *Elizabethan Language of Flowers*. ❧ During the Elizabethan era, it was customary to give one's lover different flowers to express love. ❧ Theses little bouquets were given the name "tuzzie muzzies." ❧ When a young women was given a tuzzie muzzie by her lover, she would go to the language of flowers to understand the secret message conveyed by each flower. ❧ Not all flowers expressed the finer aspects of love, but nevertheless this was the high fashion of the day. ❧

❧ Now is the time to enter the Garden of Woman's Wisdom and visualize yourself as a young girl full of innocence, yearning for love ⁄ someone who has yet to taste its nectar or know it's lessons. ❧ With this in mind, enter through the garden gate. ❧

GARDENIA

ARDENIA

Down the garden pathway we come to our first flower, the gardenia. It is a beautiful white flower so full of fragrance that it is intoxicating to the admirer. ❧ The delicate blossoms unfold for the promise of a secret lover. ❧

One of the early motivations of life is dreaming of a secret lover who will fill our needs and hopes. ❧ The young girl yearns in fantasies and daydreams for handsome male admirers. ❧

Let us acknowledge the first dew-like fantasies we have had about men. ❧

Gardenia is the flower of the secret lover. ❧

PINK
CARNATION

PINK CARNATION

Now let us feel the presence of the pink carnation. ❧ This flower symbolizes the love of the female aspect of oneself, love of our very own womanhood. ❧

What does being a woman mean to you? ❧

Rejoice in the art of being a woman. ❧ Capture the feeling side of your nature, the receptive and intuitive. ❧ Accept your body as the feminine vessel with its curves and crevices, with its sweetness and softness. ❧ Accepting your body is a important part of self love. ❧ Accept all women as the mirrors of the feminine nature. ❧

See your heart open to the female aspect, letting your heart open with self love and love towards sisterhood. ❧ Pink Carnation is the flower of self acceptance. ❧

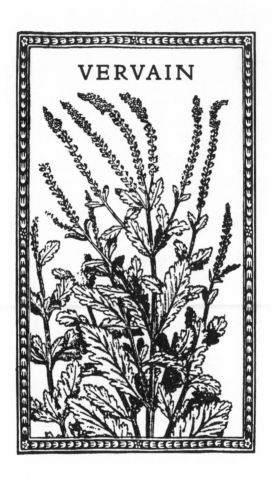

VERVAIN

VERVAIN

Vervain has little purple-blue flowers. ❧ It is an herb, whose meaning is enchantment. ❧

As we go into the world, we many times become enchanted by the men we meet. ❧

The world holds out so many delights and packages of mystery ready to be experienced through the beholder's senses. ❧

The enchantment of worldly pleasures holds major lessons that must be passed through on the pathway of life. ❧

Vervain is the flower of enchantment. ❧

WHITE LILACS

HITE LILACS

White lilacs bloom early with the first zephyrs of spring in the air. ❧ White lilacs correspond to the first emotions of love when the anticipation of seeing the lover overwhelms, and excitement tingles throughout one's whole body. ❧ It is tenderness for the first love who unlocks your heart. ❧

The first steps and experiences of love are precious. Meditate on the feeling of the first time you fell in love. ❧

White Lilacs are for the first emotions of love. ❧

PURPLE
LILACS

PURPLE LILACS

Purple Lilacs often bloom side-by-side with white lilacs as the first emotions of love stem forth from youthful innocence and trust. ❧

Purple lilacs are the innocence of a young girl who does not know the road of love, and the many pathways on which love can lead her. ❧ She is innocent to the art of loving and is following her heart. ❧

Purple Lilac is the blossom of youthful innocence. ❧

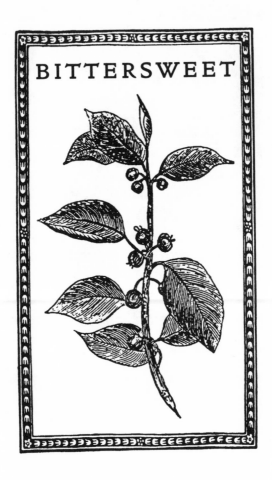

BITTERSWEET

BITTERSWEET

We now come to the place in the garden where love has paid its toll. ❧

Bittersweet symbolizes the story of lovers lost, where heartache remains.

❧ *It is when we are left alone and our heart is broken that the seed of God can be planted.* ❧

Step back and ask why the fairy tale enchantment of romantic love does not endure. ❧

Bittersweet is the disappointment of love. ❧

NARCISSUS

NARCISSUS

The next flower we pause before in the garden is Narcissus. ❧ This is the flower for overcoming ego. This flower can be as delicate as an ego; so easily overcome by the power of love. ❧ The ego builds walls around our heart to keep it from expressing love. ❧

Sometimes ego will twist and turn love to its own advantage, as in a person who uses love for selfish reasons. ❧

Sooner or later, the warmth of love will melt the hardness of ego so the heart can truly express itself. ❧

The strong yet sweet fragrance of the Narcissus is like the love which overcomes the ego, penetrating all barriers. ❧

Narcissus is the flower for melting ego. ❧

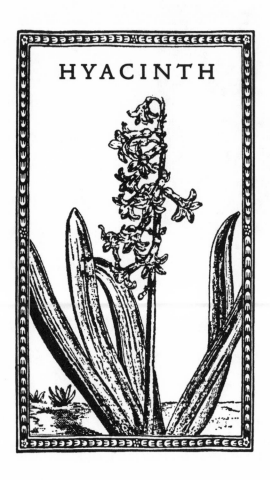

HYACINTH

HYACINTH

Moving along the garden pathway, we come to Hyacinth. ❧ *As we breathe in the essence of the waxy blossoms, we become aware of the interactions in the game of love.* ❧

We begin to see ourselves as actors playing roles in human dramas. ❧

Love becomes conquest to many of the players in the field. ❧

When we become spectators in the games of love rather than actors who must go on performing the same roles over and over, we begin to see the lessons in love. ❧

Hyacinth is the flower of the game of love. ❧

MAGNOLIA

AGNOLIA

Queenly magnolia blossoms fill the garden with their fragrance. 🌸 *Magnolias are symbolic of the force of Nature, which brings us to how Nature works in our bodies.* 🌸

As women, we have bodies which flow in natural cycles. 🌸 *When we learn the power of our cycles, we can see clearly how the force of Nature works.* 🌸

There are times during fertility that Nature's drive can be so strong we mistake passion for love. 🌸

To know our body is to understand our cycles. 🌸 *To understand cycles is to take command of the body you live in.* 🌸

Magnolia is the flower for our body's nature and its cycles. 🌸

MOCK
ORANGE

MOCK ORANGE

Orange blossoms symbolize the true bridal feast, but mock orange is the imitation of the divine marriage. ❧

Through mock orange we can learn the lessons of male and female partnership. ❧

When we work with another soul to bring life to our hopes and dreams, when we unite with another to raise children together, marriage becomes the purifying fire for our love nature. ❧

Through marriage couples spiritually united have the opportunity to realize they are the earthly expression of the divine union within the soul. ❧

Mock Orange is the human marriage. ❧

PURPLE
VIOLETS

 **URPLE VIOLETS**

Deeper in the Wisdom Garden, the fires of love begin naturally to purify the path. ❧

As the purple violet's modest flowers grow in the soil of humbleness, take pause for introspection. ❧

Just as love will lift you to the heights, it will also bring you to your knees before the Creator. ❧

Humility will reshape ego to serve a higher purpose in life. ❧

Modesty and humility may be cultivated and nurtured in one's heart by giving love. ❧

Violets remind us of humbleness and modesty. ❧

FORGET-ME-NOT

FORGET-ME-NOT

Forget-me-not blooms in sky blue for remembrance of the spiritual self. ❧

When the enchantment of the world fades because of disappointment, our search begins for deeper meaning. ❧

Still longing for union to feel complete in love, we search deeper within, until at last, we discover Spirit, watching and waiting patiently for our attention to be turned inward. ❧

Awakening from the dream, we realize that the union always desired lives within our soul. ❧

Forget-me-not is the color of remembrance. ❧

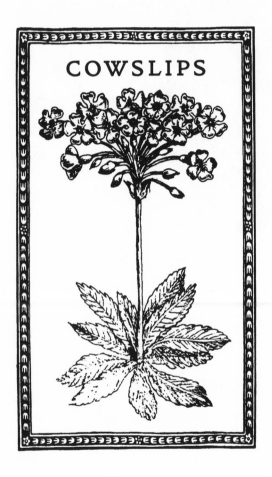

COWSLIPS

OWSLIPS

Cowslips are cultivated and grown in the soil of Divine Beauty that cannot fade with age or time. ❦ Divine Beauty is worn within. ❦ It is the beauty that comes from prayerful thoughts and kind actions. ❦

These pearls of wisdom cannot be bought or sold by the wearer, but can only be obtained by walking the path of beauty. ❦ Divine Beauty happens within the soul as we sow the seeds of forgiveness and understanding in our relationships. ❦ As we reflect upon our relationships we start to see the mirror of ourself. ❦ The separateness begins to fade, and Cowslips can begin to bloom in our garden. ❦

Cowslips are the flower of Divine Beauty. ❦

HEATHER

EATHER

Heather, with deep green leaves and tiny misty rose flowers grows in the garden as admiration for Spirit. ❧ *As the path winds nearer the Spirit of All Life, we have realizations: Spirit is everywhere and is everything.* ❧

The rose-color flowers of heather open our heart to Spirit. ❧

We understand that all our prayers can be answered by Spirit when we have faith and trust in our spiritual self. ❧ *Our devotion and admiration for Spirit grows and grows and begins to flower in the Wisdom Garden.* ❧

Heather is the stalk of admiration. ❧

STOCK

TOCK

Stocks come in many colors - white, mauve, and pink. 🌸 They grow in the soil of lasting beauty. 🌸

Heaven has a bank account, but instead of being filled with money, it is full of prayers, love, and kindness. 🌸

We become wealthy as we meditate on these spiritual virtues. 🌸 It is making an investment in our heart that time cannot take away. 🌸

Prayerful thoughts that are aligned with faith make wings to lift up the world and those around you. 🌸

The richness of stocks is seeing your prayers answered. 🌸

Stocks are the flowers of lasting beauty. 🌸

ORANGE
FLOWERS

RANGE FLOWERS

Orange Flowers bloom in the garden for the true bridal feast. ❦ *This is the union of soul and Spirit.* ❦ *God takes you as bride and lover. Nothing is more fulfilling because this is the perfect union.* ❦ *The wedding is celebrated within your heart: the realization that your own male and female aspects are unified.* ❦ *This is the everlasting love you always searched for. It is the fulfillment of the Self.* ❦ *Visualize the honeyed scent of the orange blossoms as God takes you into the bridal chamber, filling you with love so full that your cup runneth over.* ❦ *The union of True Love is complete, and with this understanding all old flames are only flickers compared to the blazing love of God.* ❦

Orange Flowers symbolize the Bridal Feast. ❦

ROSEMARY

OSEMARY

Rosemary grows and honors the Holy Mother. ❧ The division between mother and father, body and soul, is reflected in our environment, our relationships and our sexuality. ❧ This division can only be healed when we begin to accept the female aspect in ourselves and on our planet. ❧ Rosemary honors and helps us remember the Divine Feminine as we honor our environment. ❧ The feminine nature is reflected in our bodies as we listen to her and nurture ourselves through right habits, diet, and exercise. ❧ We honor our sexuality which is a reflection of the divine union that lives within us making sex sacred. ❧

Rosemary brings the remembrance of the Divine Feminine. ❧

GOLDENROD

OLDENROD

This is the scepter of freedom, the creative male force. ❧ Goldenrod stands for the energy that gives life to form in matter. ❧ As we understand we have the creative male force within, we begin to master the material world. ❧ When we align our will with God's will we can bring our projects, hopes, and dreams to completion. ❧ This male force enables us to bring our aspirations out into the world. ❧

Having the creative male energy does not mean we have to be manly or use this energy as a man would. ❧ What it does mean is that we can balance it with our feminine energy, bringing receptiveness, nurturing, and intuition to the world and our projects. ❧ Goldenrod is the scepter of freedom. ❧

WHITE ROSE

HITE ROSE

We move closer to the center of the garden and find ourselves standing before the white rose. ❧ *We gaze upon the beauty and purity the rose represents.* ❧

The white rose is our love that has been purified by the Creator or the soul's love turned towards God. ❧ *When our mind, heart, body, and soul are longing only for God's love, we become channels of Divine Will.* ❧ *Turning inward does not mean cutting off the outer world but bringing light into our daily lives to transform the world around us.* ❧

Breathe deeply the essence of the white rose, and begin to see that behind every act is the face of God and Goddess. ❧

White Rose is God's Love. ❧

ANGELICA

NGELICA

Angelica towers over the garden pathway to lead us to the Angelic Kingdom. ❧ *Angels are our unseen helpers sent from heaven.* ❧ *Each soul comes to Earth with a guardian angel to help it through earthly lessons.* ❧ *The angels are here to guard, guide, and inspire.* ❧ *Turning our attention inward, we become aware of our angels.* ❧ *Angels can only help us when we sincerely ask for their assistance. They are not allowed to interfere with a soul's free will.* ❧ *Ask now for your angel's guidance. Give permission for your angel to work with you and say a special prayer that all angels may be confirmed and blessed by God.* ❧ *Let us give thanks to God's messengers from celestial heights.* ❧

Angelica is the plant to call the Angels. ❧

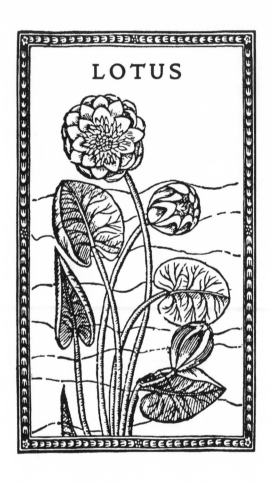

LOTUS

LOTUS

Lotus flowers float on top of a small pond in the garden, but their roots are sunk deeply into the mud of the pond. ❧

As the Lotus opens to the sunlight, each petal unfolds for wisdom and truth. ❧

Many earthly experiences are born out of the muck and mire, but we can rise above them with understanding of Divine Truth. ❧

This purity is always in each one of us. ❧ No matter what earthly lesson we have gone though, it can become the compost to grow flowers for the garden. ❧

May the Divine truth and wisdom take root in all lives. ❧

Lotus is the flower of truth. ❧

PEARLY EVERLASTINGS

PEARLY EVERLASTINGS

Pearly Everlastings represent the goal of Eternal Life. ❧

When we are fully awakened, knowing that our Spiritual Self cannot die, we claim our inheritance of everlasting life. ❧

Our purpose becomes one with God's greater plan for all humanity. ❧

Seeing ourselves as Daughters of Radiance we realize that our earth life is but a blink compared to everlasting life with God in every moment. ❧

Pearly Everlasting is the bouquet of everlasting life with God. ❧

SUNDIAL ❧ SUNDIAL ❧ SUNDIAL ❧ SUNDIAL ❧ SUNDIAL ❧ SUNDIAL ❧ SUNDIAL ❧ SUNDIAL ❧ SUNDIAL ❧ SUNDIAL ❧ SUNDIAL

We have now entered the center of the garden. ❧ From this point we clearly view all the flowers we walked with. ❧ The understanding of our experiences becomes fully visualized. ❧

The sundial reflects earthly time, but the seed of eternity has been planted in our hearts by our own work.

HE GARDEN OF WOMAN'S WISDOM AS A GROUP PROCESS

❧ For the many women participating in support groups, this book can be used as an addition or supplement to work that is already taking place. ❧ Or you might wish to form a group just to share in the Garden's process. ❧

❧ I have worked with a variety of women's groups over the years, and some of the most transcendental healings I have witnessed involved the use of flowers. ❧ Women are natural healers. ❧ Our built-in nurturing qualities make it easy for us provide the support that is such an important part of the healing process. ❧

❧ The ritual processes described below will serve women who are recovering from a divorce or a destructive relationship, as well as older women who may be having a difficult time adjusting to widowhood. ❧ The Wisdom Garden is especially well-suited as an Initiation ceremony for young girls passing into womanhood. ❧

❧ Ideally, there would be twenty-two women involved, in addition to the initiate. Each participant chooses a different flower from the mandala. ❧ Or eleven woman, each selecting two flowers. Setting the stage for the process is important. ❧ The flowers should be chosen for each woman ahead of time. ❧ This will give each person time to think about the qualities she will be bringing to the garden. ❧ Each woman might want to bring a fresh flower or a pack of flower seeds or flower essence or essential oil to the circle. ❧ Flower essences and essential oils can often be found in health food stores. ❧ One might offer a photograph or a drawing of their flower.

❧ For those who sew, embroidering the flower is a thoughtful expression. ❧ If you are in a quilting circle, each woman could make a flower block and sew them into a quilt. ❧ This makes a wonderful gift for a young girl going into womanhood or a healing gift for a special friend. ❧

❧ Each woman should bring something to the circle that creatively expresses the flower that she will be speaking for. ❧

❧ The group will need to agree on where to have the initiation. ❧ It could be in someone's home, with soft candle light and a circle of chairs. ❧ If it is spring and warm, a garden would be a perfect place. ❧ But whatever you decide, be creative and understand that you are creating a special atmosphere. ❧ The girl being initiated should wear a white dress, as if going to a wedding, the participants can dress in the color of their flower. ❧

❧ Once the group assembles, sit in the circle so the initiate can easily move around the circle to each woman who will present her flower. ❧ This process will take cooperation if more than one flower is being read by each woman. ❧

❧ All these details need to be worked out before the initiate is presented to the group. ❧ You will not want to give away the flower's messages until the initiate is presented to the group. ❧ This gives a more dramatic impact to the person who is receiving the Wisdom Garden's teachings. ❧ Sometimes it's easier to let each woman present herself and her flower's message when the initiate is seated in the center of the circle. ❧

✻ The initiation process should be explained to the initiate, along with an explanation of the mandala and how to enter the Wisdom Garden. ❧ After each woman presents her flower's message, reading the book aloud, she could also add her own wisdom she has gained from being with her flower. ❧ During the presentation keep in mind that this is a gift you are giving the initiate, presenting it in such a manner. ❧

✻ At the end of the flower message, each woman will present her fresh flower, essential oil or seed packet ⸱ whatever she has bought to represent her flower. ❧ As you go around the circle and each flower's message is read, energy will build. ❧ Do not be surprised if tears begin to flow, for this is all a part of the healing, not only for the initiate but for everyone who participates in the process. ❧ At the end, someone can crown the initiate with a flower wreath, and all join hands and celebrate her new awareness. ❧

❧ The beauty of this process is that every woman is given an opportunity to express herself uniquely though her gift and the flower's message. ❧ For the initiate it will be a time to receive the love, support and wisdom of the women in the circle. ❧ Each group will express this process in its own way. ❧

❧ I hope this book will help revive the ancient practice of initiation into womanhood and provide an initiation of healing for women. ❧

A POTPOURRI OF FLOWER KNOWLEDGE

In this section, let us go deeper into the knowledge, myth, folk wisdom and the uses of our twenty-two flowers. You also will learn the growing conditions and how to cultivate these flowers in your own garden. A few of the flowers are native wildflowers and were chosen for the Garden of Woman's Wisdom for their special meaning.

I have included recipes, and some tips that will enrich your understanding of the special qualities that each flower holds.

GARDENIA

Gardenia jasminoides

❦ Gardenia was known as the flower of the moon. ❦ Its intoxicating fragrance opens the senses to sensuality and healing. ❦ Its Latin name *jasminoides* comes from the word jasmine fragrance. ❦

❦ Gardenia needs a warm climate to flourish. ❦ It prefers the southern states and climate of the west coast. ❦ In very hot conditions it prefers filtered shade. ❦ The soil should have good drainage. ❦ You can add peat moss to the soil, to help the plant retain the moisture it thrives on. ❦

❦ The secret of growing a beautiful gardenia is regular monthly feeding before the blooming cycle. ❦ Their preferred diet consists of acid plant food, or blood meal, and fish emulsion. ❧ To grow gardenias for healing and for the Earth's sake, use organic sources for fertilizer. ❧ Gardenias can be vulnerable to chorosis, the Rx being iron sulfate. ❧ Spray for aphids with a simple solution of liquid castile soap and water. ❧ Gardenias also like to be sprayed with liquid seaweed solution to help growth. ❧ When the blooms start cracking open, just mist with water or the seaweed will stain the flowers. ❧

❧ If you grow your own or buy a single flower at the florist, nothing can scent your room like a gardenia. ❧ Floating in a bowl or pinned in your hair, no other perfume will be necessary when the gardenia is there. ❧

❧ Here are some of my favorite recipes for enjoying the scent of gardenias all year long. ❧

GARDENIA
BODY POWDER

❦ *In a wide mouth jar put in six ounces of cornstarch and one-fourth ounce of powdered Orris root. With an eyedropper add thirty to thirty-five drops of gardenia essential oil. Tightly cap the jar and put away for two weeks in a cool, dark place so the oils can incorporate with the powder.*

❦ *Remember to shake the jar periodically. After two weeks place it in a powder shaker container or powder box with puff. Use after a nice gardenia bath.*

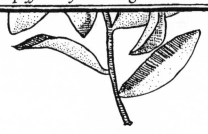

GARDENIA
BATH SALTS

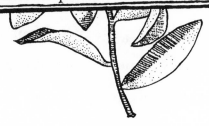

❧ In a wide mouth glass jar measure out forty ounces of Epsom salts and six ounces of sea salt and mix with a wooden chopstick. With an eyedropper add forty to forty-five drops of gardenia oil and mix into the salt then tightly cap the jar. Let the salts merge with the essential oils by putting the jar away for two weeks in cool dark place, remembering to shake it periodically. After the two weeks it is ready to use. Add two cups of the salts to your bath.

❧ You might even like to float a few fresh gardenias in your bath water. Light a candle and let the salts and oils do their magic soothing your muscles and your soul. Finish your bath with gardenia powder. Many health food stores carry essential oils, and in the herb section you will find Orris root powder. Any drug store sells Epsom salts.

PINK CARNATION

Dianthus caryophyllus

✿ The Latin name *Dianthus* means the flowers of the Gods. ✿ The genus name *caryophyllus* tells us it has a clove-like fragrance. ✿ The spicy pink carnation brings back memories of prom dresses and the first corsage. ✿ It is the flower that honors our mothers on Mother's Day. ✿

✿ Carnations are easy to grow. ✿ They like a rich garden soil and require full sun and well drained soil. ✿ You can sew the seeds directly in the garden in the spring or start as seedlings then transplant into your garden. ✿ They bloom in summer if sown in early spring. ✿

❧❋ There is a grand variety of hybrids, from Sweet Williams to Magic Charm. ❧ Keep the dead flowers trimmed. ❧ To encourage new growth use earthworm castings. ❧ This pure manure from the earthworm, is my favorite fertilizer. ❧ It can be used as a side dressing for your flowers. ❧ Purchase at plant nurseries. ❧

❧❋ Crimson Clove is one of the older varieties of carnations that has been grown in cottage gardens that date back five hundred years or more. ❧

❧❋ The Carnation can be used in your salads, cakes, and sauces. ❧ If you would like to try eating carnations, remember to cut off the heel of the petals, which has a bitter taste. ❧ Do this by plucking a few petals at a time. ❧ With little scissors, trim off the ends from the center of the flower. ❧ The petals that are left are quite edible.

✿ An herbal doctor from Mexico recommended bathing in white carnations to help release anger. ✿ He would have his patient bathe for seven days using seven white carnations in the bath water each time. ✿ The rough edges of the carnation canceled out the rough edges of anger. ✿ Bathing in carnations to release your anger, might seem a trifle strange but a few hundred years ago it was quite normal. ✿ Even today some cultures perform healing rituals with flowers. ✿

✿ Ancient people have always used and understood the healing power of plants and modern man is rediscovering their healing qualities.

✿ Here are a few more ideas for putting carnations to work for you:

CARNATION
MASSAGE OIL

❦ For this recipe I use an earthenware pot that holds at least a pint. If you are growing carnations in your garden. pick them early in the morning after the dew has dried. Just use the petals and fill the jar at least half-full of flowers. Now drizzle sweet almond oil over the petals, just covering the top of the flowers. Cover the jar with a clean piece of cheese cloth and secure it with a rubber band. Place the jar in a safe, sunny space. The earthenware jar absorbs the heat of the sun to help warm the oil. The cheese cloth lets the oil breath so it will not collect moisture from the flowers. You can strain the flowers out at the end of the day making sure you squeeze the flowers with the back of a wooden spoon . I like to use a strainer lined with cheese cloth so the oil comes out clean. If you want to make a stronger flower oil repeat the process the next day using the same oil and adding fresh flowers . This can be repeated several times to intensify the scent of the oil. When finished strain the oil several times though cheese cloth and pour in clean glass jars and label. This oil will last much longer if it is refrigerated.

❦ This same method can be used with other scented flowers or highly scented herbs. You also can mix several different flowers in one oil mixture.

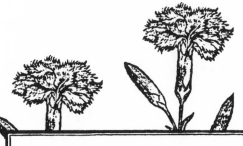

CARNATION HONEY

❧ To a pint of orange blossom honey or any light tasting honey add three flowers of carnations D. caryophyllus. Remember to cut off the heels before adding flowers to the honey. Use a clear glass jar and let the mixture sit in a sunny window for three days .

❧ You can serve this honey at tea time or even dab it on your face for a quick flower facial. Spread the carnation honey on your face, remembering to avoid the soft tissue beneath the eyes. Massage the skin using your finger tips. When the honey becomes tacky pull your fingers away from your skin. Do this all over your face. This stimulates the blood circulation and gives a nice glow to the skin. Rinse off, making sure honey is out of your hair line and eyebrows.

VERVAIN
Verbena officinalis

❧ I remember coming across Vervain in an open wildflower field in up-state New York. ❧ Its steeple shaped purple flowers poked though the tall summer grasses. ❧ In the Language of Flowers it means enchantment. ❧

❧ I grow this herb in my garden now and use the tea to help soothe nerves. ❧ Its as-tringent qualities have been used to wash and heal wounds. ❧ Its Latin name means sacred bough and *officinalis* means 'from the pharmacopoeia' or, in simpler terms, it is medicinal. ❧

❧ Vervain grows wild by roadsides in open fields and waste places. ❧ It likes limestone soil. It has lance shaped leaves and spiky purple flowers. ❧ It grows one to three feet tall. ❧ It came from Europe but escaped from the early settler's gardens and adapted itself to the wilds. ❧ You can easily grow it from seed, or divide it from root cuttings. ❧ It likes a sunny garden plot and well drained soil. ❧

❧ The early Romans consecrated their temples with this herb. ❧ The Egyptians saw it as the tears of Isis, the goddess who mourned her husband Osiris. ❧ The Druids wove and wore crowns of Vervain and the Pagans used it to protect themselves during rituals. ❧ The Christians claimed that it was the herb used to stop the bleeding of Christ's wounds during the crucifixion. ❧

❧ Vervain contains glycoside, which can cause vomiting taken it large doses. ❧ One cup of tea is all you ever need for stress or nervousness. ❧

MELLOW OUT TINCTURE WITH VERVAIN

- ❧ *one pint of vodka*
- ❧ *one-third to one pint each of vervain, skullcap, and passionflower*

❧ This tincture is very good for stress or insomnia. It can be taken from an eyedropper three times a day.

❧ I like to use fresh herbs from my garden to create this tincture but when not available, dried herbs can be used. Finely chop the herbs vervain, passionflower, and skullcap and pack loosely into pint jar leaving enough room at the top of the jar to pour liquid. Now pour vodka over the herbs making sure that you cover the herbs completely. Cap the jar and shake. Place in cool dark place and remember to shake daily. I like my tincture to soak for six weeks at the very least. More often I leave the herbs to soak for three months. This makes the medicine strong and effective. Strain the herbs from the vodka making sure that you squeeze the herbs with the back of a wooden spoon so that all the oils and medicine are in the tincture. You now might want to strain the tincture once more through several layers of cheese cloth. You can now bottle your tincture in clean eyedropper bottles. Label and use when needed. This tincture can be very strong, only use when it is really needed.

VERVAIN TEA

❧ One teaspoon of vervain to one cup of hot, boiled water. Steep five minutes, sip slowly, and feel yourself relax.

WHITE AND PURPLE LILACS
Syringa vulgaris

Lilacs evoke sentimental memories for me. Often a scent will remind you of past events in your life. My grandmother always thought of her mother when the Lilacs bloomed because they were blooming the day her mother died. Lilacs remind me of my daughter's birth because they were in full bloom when she was born. Nostalgia and Lilacs seem to go hand in hand.

I've always loved to make herbal cosmetics and use flowers to soothe the spirit. Many years ago I conducted a healing day for women at a beautiful bathhouse on the slopes of California's sacred Mt. Shasta.

❧ Many of us were young mothers, and the idea of taking time out for ourselves was a novel idea. ❧ I used herbs and flowers to make this day special. ❧ The sauna had sizzling herbal oils on the rocks. The cold plunge was covered with freshly picked wild mint. ❧ The bath house with its sunken hot tub was beautifully made. ❧ Stained glass windows all around allowed the sun to stream through the windows, making color patterns on the wall. ❧ But it was the pounds of fresh lilac flowers that floated on top of six hundred gallons of herbal bath that sent everyone straight to heaven. ❧

GROWING LILACS

❦ *Syringa means lilac in Latin, and vulgaris comes from the word vulgar meaning common.*

❦ *Lilacs like the colder climates, but some types can be grown in warmer regions. They require alkaline soil, and if your soil is too acidic, lime should be added and dug deeply into the soil.*

❦ *You should shape lilacs in the tree's early years by pinching the leaves back. The flower buds grow in pairs and can be found where leaves join the stem for the next year's growth. Over-pruning lilacs can inhibit the next years blooming. Scale is sometimes a problem. In rare cases leaf mold or downy mildew can be a problem.*

❦ *Syringa vulgaris can reach up to twenty feet tall. It takes two to three years for lilacs to produce full size flowers and true colors.*

LILAC SPRING BATH

- One gallon of spring water
- One cup of each; chamomile, linden, elder flowers, and rose petals
- A basket of freshly picked lilacs

Heat the spring water in stainless steel pot and when it boils take off the heat and add the chamomile, linden, elderflowers, and rose petals. Cover and let steep overnight. The next morning after pouring your bath strain your herbal brew into the bath water. Place the leftover herbs into a wash cloth, gathering the ends, secure with a rubber band, and place in the bath water. This can be used as an herbal wash cloth. Float the fresh Lilies in the bath water and get ready to experience Spring

BITTERSWEET NIGHT SHADE

Solanum dulcamara L.

🌿 Bittersweet does not have a very good reputation in the plant kingdom. 🌿 The whole plant is highly poisonous. 🌿 It is of the nightshade family, an unfriendly relative of the tomato and potato. 🌿

🌿 It is a perennial and likes to grow in damp places along stream beds. 🌿

🌿 Bittersweet was naturalized from Europe. 🌿 It is a vine that can grow up to ten feet tall and has heart shaped leaves with two ear-shaped leaves at the base of each heart. 🌿 Its attractive purple flowers and red fruit have lured many young children into tasting it. 🌿 The purple star-like flowers have bright yellow stamens. 🌿 The

Latin name *dulcamara* relates to the bitter sweet taste of it's fruit. ❧

❧ It was the sacred herb of Atropos, the Greek Goddess, whose job was cutting the thread of life for souls passing though the porthole of death. ❧

❧ It was placed under the pillow to help one forget a lost lover. ❧

❧ Herbalists of long ago used this plant for skin diseases and treatment of sores. Scientists have found that extracts of this plant can help inhibit the growth of tumors. ❧

❧ This is one plant I would not grow in my garden. ❧ Though beautiful to look at, I personally prefer its cousin the Tomato. ❧

NARCISSUS

Narcissus tazetta

One of the best known flower myths is the one of Narcissus, the foolish youth who had eyes only for himself. He liked to visit a reflecting pond and admire his own image in the water. A water nymph named Echo, fell hopelessly in love with him. One day Narcissus tried in vain to embrace his own image, falling into the pond to his death. In her grief Echo joined by her sisters tried to save Narcissus but couldn't find his body. All they found was a small fragrant flower floating on top of the pond. Echo, broken hearted, wasted away to nothing, but her voice that can still be heard in lonely and deserted places calling for her lost lover.

✗✳In some cultures Narcissus is also known as the New Year flower because it is force bloomed to open on New Year's Day. ❧ This flower is poisonous, and that quality does makes it deer resistant in your flower garden. ❧ It is a hardy cold climate flower and its bulbs will increase year after year when planted in the garden. ❧ Its leaves are flat and straight. ❧ The petals grow in a ring of right angles. ❧ It's fragrance is sweet and heady. ❧

✗✳When planting bulbs outside in your garden, add bone meal or bulb food to increase the vigor of the bloom. ❧

NARCISSUS FOR NEW YEARS

❧ *You must start your bulbs six weeks before you want them to bloom. If you are thinking about Christmas presents or New Year's Day don't wait until the last moment. Buy Dutch bulbs. They are the finest quality on the market. You can usually find bulb pots or interesting bowls where you buy your bulbs. Check out garage sales for china bowls or glass containers. You also will need small polished black pebbles and horticultural sand.*

❧ *In a container pour about one and one half inches of sand on the bottom. Now add a thin layer of black pebbles and sand. Fitting as many bulbs that you can in your container arrange with the tip of the bulb upright, then add more pebbles around the bulbs securing them in place. Add water, keep in cool, dark place until the growth is well along, making sure the bulbs always have water in their bowl. When the leaves are well established bring them into a sunny window to develop the blooms.*

❧ *Do not keep in a hot room or they will bloom quickly and fade. In cooler rooms the flowers last longer.*

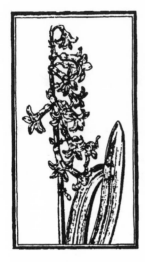

HYACINTH
Hycinthus orientalis

✿ Hyacinthus was the son of Amyclas the King of Sparta and also the beloved friend of Apollo, the God of the sun. ❧ Zephyr was the god of the wind and he was very jealous of Apollo's relationship with Hycinthus. ❧ One day Apollo and Hycinthus were playing a game of quoits. ❧ When Apollo threw his quoit, Zephyr made a gust of wind that turned the quoit towards Hyacinthus and it struck him dead. ❧ From the blood of Hycinthus the flower was born. ❧

✿ The myths and flower legends were told by the ancients to demonstrate lessons. ❧ Many of the stories were adapted and re-adapted as each culture faded into another.

❧ Many of the stories or the Latin names will reveal the healing secrets the flower might offer to humankind. ❧

❧ Hyacinth is another inedible flower, but you can inhale as much of it's fragrance as you like. ❧ Its sweet waxy blossoms and engulfing fragrance are sure signs that spring has arrived. ❧

GROWING HYACINTH

❧ *All climate zones are suitable to grow hyacinth but it does prefer cold climates. It has bell shaped flowers that grow in spike formation. The spikes emerge from a bundle of narrow green leaves. They have waxy blossoms that come in purple, white, and pink. ❧ When planting hyacinth in your garden, plant them in groups of three, five, or seven. Remember to use bone meal or bulb food. After blooming, water the bulbs until the leaves turn yellow and die back. The chlorophyll of the leaves will feed the bulb for next year's growth.*

HYACINTH VASE FOR INDOOR FLOWERING

❦ *The autumn months are the time to purchase hyacinth bulbs for indoor winter flowering. Purchase your bulbs and a special hyacinth vase made for growing bulbs in water. The vase is filled with water and small pebbles. Now place the bulb roots down into the vase. Fill with water until it touches the base of the bulb. Keep in cool dark place until roots are well established. Do not let the water level get low. When the top leaves appear, place bulb vase in sunny window. The leaves will turn green and very soon the head of the flower will appear for an indoor winter bloom.*

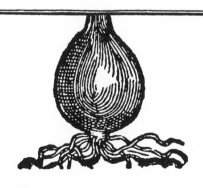

MAGNOLIA
Magnolia grandiflora

Magnolia grandiflora is true to its name, for the flowers are a grand size compared with others in the garden. The tree can grow up to eighty feet but it's distinctive blooms only appear after fifteen years. Grafted trees or cuttings from mature magnolia trees can bloom in two to three years. Its pure white flowers measure eight to ten inches across and their full body fragrance fills the air on summer afternoons. Its leaves are leathery and glossy. It is evergreen and makes a good lawn or street tree.

Folklore speaks of placing magnolias under your pillow to keep your mate faithful. Images of Southern Bells sipping mint juleps are the visions this old favorite brings to mind. ❧

❧ Floating magnolias in glass bowls and bringing them into your house during summer is a beautiful way to bring the fragrance indoors. ❧

DRYING MAGNOLIA BLOSSOMS

❧ In a clean shoe box put in one cup of Borax hand soap and five cups of cornmeal and mix thoroughly. Cut fresh magnolia blossoms one or two at a time and bury in the borax cornmeal mixture. Arrange the magnolia with the stem up and blossom face down in the cornmeal mixture and then bury the back of the flower. Cover the shoe box with its top and place in a cool dry place. In a few weeks, test to see if the blossoms are dry. They will be crisp to the touch. This same method can also be used to dry other flowers you might like to preserve.

MAGNOLIA MILK BATH

- 🌼 one gallon of water
- 🌼 one cup of each rose petals, rosemary, lavender, lemon balm
- 🌼 two cups powdered milk
- 🌼 four of five freshly picked magnolia blossoms

🌼 In a stainless steel pot add spring water and bring to a boil. Only use stainless steel or glass when making herbal medicines. Take off the heat and add just the rose petals, rosemary, lavender, and lemon balm. Cover the pot with a lid and let the herbs steep overnight. In the morning freshly pick the magnolia blossoms. Begin to pour your bath straining the herbal brew into the bath water. Then add the powdered milk to the bath and stir with your hands. Float the magnolias in the bath. Light some candles, put on some soft music and take a bath fit for a queen.

MOCK ORANGE

Philadelphus lewisi

Mock orange is in the hydrangea family. The *Philadelphus lewisi* is native to North America. Its wood has been used by Native American tribes in Northern California for pipe stems and arrow shafts. The Klamath River Indians use the Mock Orange in a ceremonial dance that initiates young girls into womanhood. The pithy stem of the mock orange was easily sliced and made into an object much like a small broom or wood flower. This became the ceremonial tool used for the young virgins initiation in the flower dance. The elder woman of the tribe would pray and teach the girls what they would need to know to become women. ❧This ceremonial dance is now being rejuvenated by some of the traditional women in the Klamath Tribes. ❧

❧ Mock Orange has a very sweet satiny fragrance. ❧The blooms can be two inches across and the leaves are oval. ❧ It blooms in June and July and is the state flower of Idaho. ❧ Its growing habit is arching and erect. ❧ It grows wild on rocky slopes or mixed woodland area. ❧ It is a good native for gardening in the western states because of its drought tolerant qualities. ❧

MOCK ORANGE TALKING STICK

❧ In all marriages, communication is important for a healthy relationship. The Native Americans have the beautiful tradition of the talking stick. The stick is used so each person has a chance to fully express themselves without interruptions. When the person is holding the stick no one else can speak until the stick is passed to the next person. This method is used in the family and the tribe, so that each person's view point is heard and listened to.

❧ In the Garden of Wisdom, mock orange symbolizes the human marriage. What better way to use this plant than for healing the communication between the sexes.

❧ Obtain a stick of mock orange about 12 inches long. If you are picking it from nature, please do so with respect for the plant and the natural environment. The stick can be wrapped with colored yarns, decorated with beads, or even carved. You can even make a special bag to put your stick in. Making a mock orange talking stick should be a creative process between partners.

❧ When those times come in marriage that communication becomes difficult and you aren't listening to each other, bring out the talking stick and remember the process and the purpose of making this stick; then sit down, communicate, and listen to each other.

FORGET-ME-NOT

Myosotis scorpiodes

⚘ Forget-Me-Not is surrounded by folklore and legends that are filled with the sweet senti-ments of lovers. ⚘ An old European story tells of a handsome knight who was asked by his lady to pick these flowers. ⚘ As he picked the little blue flowers by the river's edge he slipped and fell into the swift current. ⚘ Since he couldn't swim he called out to his lady be-fore his last breath, "forget me not." ⚘ In the Language of Flowers, Forget-Me-Not means true love cannot be forgotten. ⚘

⚘ Forget-me-not flowers were native to Europe but became easily naturalized in many parts of North America. ⚘ They can grow up to two feet tall. Its little blue flowers stretch across a hairy stem that turns into a spiral at it's tip. ❧ This trait inspired its Latin name *Scorpiodes* after the scorpion's tail. ❧ Forget-Me-Not is the herbal medicine for healing scorpion bites, bee stings, and venomous bites. ❧ It also had the folk name of Scorpion Grass. ❧ It spreads by its root system but can be easily grown from seed. ❧ Once established in the garden it will return year after year with little care. ❧

❧ Its scorpion tail feature was the reason King Henry of England choose it for his emblem. ❧ Henry was booted out the country in 1398 by cousin Richard, who was king at the moment. ❧ Henry vowed to return, and return he did, with this flower leading the war. ❧ As for poor Richard, he ended up in prison, the victim of the scorpion tail. ❧

BEE STING POULTICE

❦ Is it not poetic that scorpiodes makes a potion that relieves the sting? You will need a mortar and pestle and a handful of fresh leaves of forget-me-nots

❦ Place fresh forget-me-not leaves in the mortar and grind into a green paste. Place this paste on bee sting, bandage to keep poultice secure and leave it on one hour or more.

PURPLE VIOLETS
Viola odorata

✿ The green heart shaped leaves and deep purple flowers of Violet often go unnoticed on the garden pathway. ✿ But true to its Latin name *odorata,* this meek flower sweetens a garden. ✿

✿ The fragrant Sweet Violet is usually found in the shade, but it doesn't mind basking in the early morning sun. ✿ The plant grows from two to eight inches. ✿ It requires well drained soil. ✿ You can sow the seeds of Violets in rich moist soil. ✿ Or you can divide plants at the crown remembering to detach the plant's runners. ✿

✿ The flowers are edible and are a nice touch for a spring salad or garnished on a casserole dish. ❧ Violet flowers have a calming effect when made into a sweet syrup. ❧ They have been used in herbal medicine as a child's laxative. ❧

❧ The Greeks honored the Blue Violets, believing they calmed tempers and helped one to have a good night's sleep. ❧ In Rome, garlands were woven and placed on the head as a headache cure. ❧ Fresh leaves of Violets have been used since ancient times to cure tumors and growths, but modern science has been unable to prove that it is effective. ❧

❧ Sweet Violet water was most likely one of your great grandmother's boudoir articles. ❧ It's popularity is making a comeback with the new interest in aromatherapy. ❧

VIOLET CRYSTALIZED CANDY

- 🌸 one egg
- 🌸 a basket of fresh clean violets
- 🌸 one cup of superfine white sugar
- 🌸 toothpicks
- 🌸 a lump of clay

🌸 Pick your violets in the morning, after the dew has dissipated. Then separate the yolk from one egg and set aside. I like to destem the violets and put a toothpick in the place of the stem. This ensures that the violets will dry properly. Dip the toothpick violet into the egg white and gently roll it in white sugar. Then place the sugar violets toothpick into the lump of clay so that the sugar coated violet can dry on all sides. It sometimes takes a day or two for violets to dry, depending on the weather and humidity. After the flowers have dried, store them in a box, placing clean tissue paper between layers so the flowers do not stick. These candies can be simply eaten, or used to decorate a cake or tea cookies.

SPRING POWER AND VIOLET SPREAD

- ❧ *one-half pound of tofu*
- ❧ *one cup of finely chopped parsley*
- ❧ *three cloves of garlic finely chopped*
- ❧ *one cup of fresh picked violet flowers*
- ❧ *one-half cup of olive oil*
- ❧ *soy sauce and cayenne for taste*
- ❧ *one-half cup sunflower seeds*
- ❧ *one cup of freshIy picked chickweed (Stellaria Media) This herb likes dark moist places and usually can be found growing wild in your garden. You may be pulling it up as weeds!*

❧ I love spring time, and all the new plants that can be eaten. The chlorophyll content is at its peak. This spread can be used as a dip or open face sandwich.

❧ Pick the chickweed, violet flowers, and parsley and bring home and wash. In a blender add tofu oil, and garlic and blend. Chop the parsley and chickweed and slowly add to the blender, blending as you go along. The sunflower seeds, soy sauce, and cayenne are blended next. Serve this green spread in a bowl covered with fresh violet flowers. It can be spread on crackers or bread decorated with Violets.

HEATHER
Calluna vulgaris L.

Driving to the coast on a cool February morning we turned the corner and saw the most beautiful hill all in bloom with purple pink blossoms of Heather. Of course I couldn't help myself. I stopped the car to walked though this blooming Heather field. No, I was not on the coast of Scotland. I was in Northern California, where the Heather was being cultivated for the flower market. I am sure the experience was quite similar to seeing the Scottish moors abloom with Heather.

Heather has been used in the British Isles to make brooms and thatched roofs. In Scotland, where the wool industry prides itself on its craft, Heather is used as a natural dye, giving honey brown hues to their woolens. ❧

❧ White Heather is a sign of good luck and many old bridal bouquets have had a sprig tucked into it for just this reason. ❧ It was used as a charm to bring rain to parched fields. ❧ It also was carried by women to keep them safe from rape when traveling alone. ❧

❧ Heather has been naturalized in North America. ❧ It grows as far north as Newfoundland. ❧ It likes sandy soil and prefers the coastal areas. ❧ It is an evergreen scrub with needle like leaves that grow to about one eighth inch. ❧ The scrub grows up to two feet tall in the wild. ❧

❧ Ancient herbalists used heather tea for cough medicine and to help induce sleep. ❧

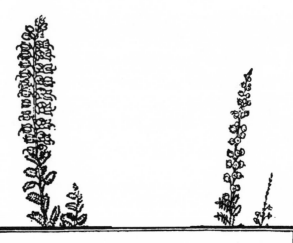

HEATHER TEA FOR COUGHS

🌿 *One teaspoon of heather blossoms to one cup of hot boiled water.*

🌿 *Steep five minutes and strain. Pour into tea cup and add one teaspoon of honey to help soothe the throat.*

STOCKS
Matthiola

Stocks were used as a part of many old fashioned flower gardens. When I lived on the East Coast, I had a beautiful circle garden where I cultivated about 150 different herbs and flowers. The frost came and went but the lovely Stocks lived on thriving until the winter cold really set in. Stocks have a sweet fragrance that sometimes catches my nose when I least expect it. I love the beauty these old time favorites bring to my garden. The Language of Flowers says Stocks are symbolic for lasting beauty. They are one of the last bloomers in my fall garden. Stocks come in an assortment of pastel colors. They have long narrow gray green leaves, and their flower stalks stand erect with clusters of blossoms. ❧ They require cooler temperatures. ❧ Plant in the early spring or late summer for fall blooming. ❧ They are biennials but are sold in nurseries as annuals. ❧ They need fertile soil and full sun to perform. ❧ Plant six to eight inches apart. ❧

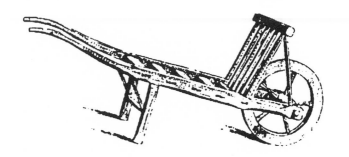

STOCK TUZZY MUZZY

❧ *A Tuzzy Muzzy is small bouquet of flowers surrounded with lace and ribbons and given to friends and loved ones. I love to go to my garden and gather flowers and make these small bouquets with scraps of lace and ribbons. Gather one white rose for the center of the bouquet, adding color stocks around the rose. I like to have a scented herb like Santolina for the border of the bouquet. Working around in a circle, secure the flowers with florist tape at the stems when you have the arrangement to your liking. Place the bouquet in water and set aside. Now take two feet of white lace about two inches wide and gather at one side with needle and thread. Pull together, arranging the gathers around the bouquet. Sew the lace ends together. Add color ribbons and tie bows. Place in a small vase and give to your friend.*

ORANGE FLOWERS

Citrus sinensis

Orange Blossoms have graced many a bridal bouquet. The sweetness of their scent speaks of Chastity in the Language of Flowers. In the nineteenth century Orange Blossoms were at their peak of popularity for a new bride. Queen Victoria carried these fragrant flowers on her own wedding day.

Roman mythology tells the story of Jupiter gifting his new wife Juno with Orange Blossoms.

Orange trees are evergreen and are prized for their fruit. They have green glossy leaves and require hotter climates to grow. They do not tolerate frost and may need to be protected in winter during cold snaps, even in southern climates. ❧

❧ They should be fertilized three times a year with a natural product that is high in nitrogen, large quantities of phosphorus, and potash. ❧ They can suffer from iron chlorosis, or lack of zinc. ❧ This can show up as yellow leaves with dark veins. ❧ Zinc deficiency is detected by blotchy yellow leaves. ❧ To correct this condition, treat the tree with iron sulfate or iron. ❧

❧ Flowers usually bloom from February to April, ready for any Spring Bride. ❧

❧ Orange Flowers can be used in potpourris and can be added to roses. ❧ Orange Flower water can be used as a facial splash to refine the complexion. ❧

NEROLI OIL SCENTED BATH (ORANGE FLOWERS)

❧ *Many women have busy lives and do not have time for making an herbal bath to relax in. This bath is for those of you who have little time. Pour your bath water, add two capfuls of a natural shampoo, and ten drops of Neroli oil. Fill a wash cloth with one cup of oatmeal, gathering the end and securing with rubber band. Place the oatmeal cloth in the tub, and use the oatmeal washcloth to scrub your skin as you soak This bath not only softens your skin, but releases stress and tension.*

ROSEMARY

Rosmarinus officinalis

Rosemary is a Mediterranean shrub that can grow to six feet. It is entwined with folk wisdom and religious lore. There is a story that Rosemary originally had white flowers but a colorful miracle was performed to change the hue of the flowers. Mary, Joseph, and the Baby Jesus were traveling to Egypt to escape King Herod. They stopped to rest. Mary washed the swaddling clothes of the Christ Child and hung them out to dry on a nearby Rosemary bush. The flowers were so honored that they blushed the color of the Madonna's blue mantle. Even to this day the Rosemary bush never grows taller then the height of Christ, and will bow its branches down to honor the Master. ❧ This plant bears the name of Mary and her symbolic flower the Rose. ❧ *Rosmarinus* means "fond of the sea," for its natural habitat is by the Mediterranean Sea. ❧

❧ It was used to retain memories. ❧ In ancient Greece, students wore it in their hair to help them study. ❧ Brides stuck a sprig in their bouquets to honor the family they were leaving behind. ❧

❧ It is a hardy evergreen scrub that can be grown from seed, but its growth is much faster when you propagate cuttings. ❧ It needs a light, well drained soil, and full sun. ❧ In colder climates you should bring Rosemary indoors for the winter. ❧ It makes lovely Christmas trees or center piece decorations when potted. ❧ Rosemary lends itself well for shaping into hedges. ❧ Traditionally it was often grown with Lavender as a hedge for monastic gardens. ❧

❧ Down though the ages herbalists have used it for sore muscles, gout, lost memory, headache, facial steams, hair rinse, cosmetics, digestive strengtheners, and as an antiseptic ⸱ the original "cure⸱all." ❧

❧ Rosemary found its way into the modern kitchen because of its superb flavor in soups and meat dishes. ❧

❧ Shakespeare writes of it in his sonnet: "There's Rosemary that's for remembrance, pray, love, remember." ❧

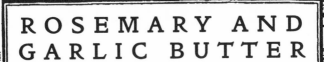

ROSEMARY AND GARLIC BUTTER

- *one cup of unsalted butter*
- *Four to six cloves of finely chopped garlic*
- *three T of finely chopped rosemary*

Let the butter soften at room temperature and place in a glass bowl. Blend rosemary and garlic together into the softened butter. For interesting shapes I use simple cookie cutters as my butter molds. You can also use a small bowl for a mound shape. Place the herbal butter in your mold and put in the refrigerator to harden. After the butter has hardened remove from the mold. You can decorate the top of the butter with blue rosemary flowers or if you are working with the mound shape you can weave a small circle of rosemary sprigs and place it on the top of your butter. Be creative! Serve with dinner rolls or hot homemade bread.

ROSEMARY AND HERBS CREAM CHEESE SPREAD

- ❧ *one large packet of cream cheese*
- ❧ *three finely chopped garlic cloves*
- ❧ *three T's of fresh rosemary finely chopped*
- ❧ *three T's of oregano finely chopped*
- ❧ *one-fourth cup of parsley finely chopped*
- ❧ *one T of sage finely chopped*
- ❧ *one cup of sunflower seeds*

❧ *This spread tastes like a fancy gourmet cheese but it's just cream cheese with freshly picked herbs. Those of you who are watching your waist line can also use low-fat cream cheese.*

❧ *Blend all the ingredients together except the sunflower seeds. Now mold, with your clean hands, a round ball from the cheese mixture. Place the cup of sunflower seeds on a plate and roll the cheese ball into the seeds covering all the sides. Put the cheese ball on a plate, cover with wrap and put in the refrigerator overnight, this gives time for the herbs flavor to blend with the cream cheese. Serve on a plate. I like to decorate the cheese ball with edible flowers like Johnny jump ups, calendula, rosemary flowers or carnation petals.*

ROSEMARY LAVENDER VINEGAR

❧ I love to clean my house with herbal vinegars. I use them on everything, drain boards, tables, kitchen floors, and bathrooms. You can even rinse your hair with it if you dilute two capfuls of herbal vinegar to one cup of water.

❧ Fresh sprigs of rosemary, lavender, sage. and thyme. Pour a little of the vinegar out of the bottle not very much, you do not want it to overflow when you add the herbs. Place the sprigs of fresh herbs in the vinegar directly in the bottle. Place vinegar in a sunny window or outside in the summer sun and let steep for two weeks. I clean everything with this safe and fragrant cleaning product. Just put some on your sponge and go to work.

COWSLIPS
Primula veris

🌾 Cowslips were known as Lady's Keys or Keys of Heaven. ❧ Many of the flowers that use the name Lady, refer to flowers for the Blessed Mother Mary. ❧ The churches of Europe dedicated many flowers to Mary, but some of the same flowers might have been dedicated to Venus or other Goddesses before the coming of Christianity. ❧ This flower still holds the name Lady reminding us to honor the Holy Mother. ❧

🌾 Cowslips in folklore were the treasure finders. ❧ It was believed that holding a bunch of Cowslips would help you find a hidden treasure. ❧ In the Language of Flowers the meaning is Divine Beauty. ❧

Truly this is a treasure to be enjoyed. ✺

✺ Cowslips were referred to by Shakespeare in *Mid Summers Night Dream* as a potion to make one beautiful. ✺ The leaves were used as a wrinkle cream in herbal cosmetics and Cowslips were served as a tea to prevent headaches and gout. ✺

✺ Cowslips have bright yellow flowers and you will find their heads poking out of moist soil in the early spring. ✺ The flowers are about one-half inch in size, and can grow from four to eight inches tall. ✺ In warmer climates cowslips can be used as a winter color. ✺

COWSLIP SCRUB
TO KEEP ONE
FAIR OF FACE

❧ Place one cup of uncooked oatmeal, one-fourth cup of almonds and half a cup of dry cowslip flowers in a blender or coffee grinder. Grind the oatmeal into a fine powder and place in a bowl. Now grind the almonds into a fine powder and stir into the oatmeal. Grind the cowslip blossoms into powder, stirring them into the oatmeal and almonds. Place in a clean glass jar and cap. Now when you want to use this magical scrub just put a small amount in your hand and add enough water to make a paste and gently scrub your face. You can leave it on your face until it is dry, then rinse off with cool water and pat dry.

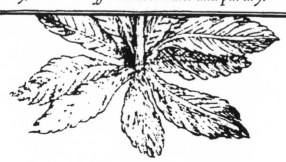

GOLDENROD
Solidago ordora

For years Goldenrod has taken the blame for many people who suffer from hay fever. However it is not Goldenrod that sends its golden pollen on the wind to cause this irritation, but its country cousin Ragweed that blooms along side Goldenrod during hay fever season.

Goldenrod was known as Liberty Tea to the American colonist. It was one of the tea substitutes used during the time of the Boston Tea Party to avoid the onerous tea tax. It is likely the early settlers had learned the Indian example of drinking this tea for intestinal disorders and colic.

Goldenrod also is used as a natural dye

source bringing its golden yellow color to woolens and cloth. ❧ It's country name was Aaron's Rod. ❧

❧ Legend has it that if you wore a sprig you might see your future beloved. ❧

❧ Goldenrod blooms in the late summer and fall. Its habitat is dry and it loves the open fields. ❧ It is native to the United States. ❧ It grows twenty to forty inches high. ❧ Its leaves are slender and smooth and can be as far as five inches from the stock. ❧ Its yellow flower heads grow on arching branches. ❧ Goldenrod can be found in some plant nurseries. ❧ It is used for planting in meadows and as a colorful summer garden border. ❧ It grows well with Black Eyed Susan and Asters. ❧ It grows best if you do not use a rich soil. ❧ Goldenrod likes full sun and average water. ❧

L I B E R T Y   T E A

❧ *One teaspoon of goldenrod flowers per cup of hot water. Steep until golden. You can add honey to sweeten.*

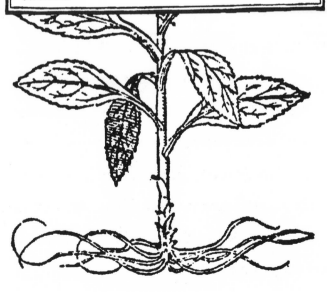

WHITE ROSE
Rosa alba

When we think of roses we think of love and romance but the White Rose suggests love that has been turned to God. Roses have been celebrated and cultivated for centuries. They have honored the Goddess Venus, and they are enshrined in prayers to the Virgin Mary. They are given to lovers often as tokens of affection. No flower has spoken to the human soul as much as the Rose.

In ancient Rome, the White Rose was hung on the ceiling over a feast to let everyone know that what took place there would not be spoken of outside of the room. It was used as a code of silence, even in the cathedrals. The White Rose would be carved over the confessional, symbolizing the oath of silence that each priest takes on hearing confessions. ❧

❧ Roses have been used by herbalists for treatments of eyes, skin, stomach for and cosmetics. ❧ Natural vitamin C tablets contain the valued rosehips. ❧

❧ The *Rosa alba* is a beautiful scented rose. ❧ It grows taller then many other roses and has fewer thorns. ❧ The wood is green and smooth and the leaves are gray green. ❧ The flower petals are semidoubled and very fragrant. ❧

❧ I have been growing roses organically. ❧ Although many experts feel this can't be done, I have found a way to have beautiful blooms without using harmful poison. ❧

RUST, MOLD, APHID, AND BLACK SPOT ROSE SPRAY

❧ *In a one gallon of water add two tablespoons of baking soda, two teaspoons of light cooking oil, and two tablespoons of liquid Castile soap. Stir all together and put in a spray bottle. Remove all the infected leaves that are on the rose stem and pick up all dead leaves that have fallen on to the ground. If the entire plant is infected remove only three fourths of the leaves. Now spray the plants, remembering also to spray underneath the leaves. If you do not have aphids, omit the soap in the recipe. If you do not have black spot, rust, or mold, but have aphids, omit the baking soda. I have found that a weekly spraying during the spring keeps my roses blooming and healthy.*

FEEDING THE ROSES

❧ *I also feed the roses in the spring every six weeks with bat guano until the buds start to form. After the buuds arrive, I switch to a balanced organic rose food. In the winter, use bone meal for root and stem development every six weeks. This will bring wonderfully healthy blooms in Spring.*

WHITE ROSE AND WHITE CLAY FACIAL

- ❦ one-fourth cup off cosmetic white clay
- ❦ one cup of dried white rose petals, any larger petal rose can be used or any color
- ❦ one good friend

❦ Now that you know how to grow organic Roses you can put them to good use. You will need a friend to help put on this facial. It takes time but it is well worth the effort. Start with a clean face. Use two small bowls putting clay in one and the rose petals in the other. Boil a small amount of water and pour just over the rose petals to cover. Set aside and let cool.

❦ Add enough warm water to the white clay to make a thin paste. The person receiving the facial lies down using a towel to cover the floor so things don't get too messy. The friend now applies the white clay to the face making sure that the neck is covered in upward strokes. Avoid the under-eye area where the skin is very sensitive. Take the bowl of white rose petals, taking a petal at a time: gently spread each petal flat and place it on the clay mask. Cover the face and neck one petal at time until you get a mosaic effect. The petal facial can also be done with red and white roses which is very beautiful when completed. Let the facial dry, then peel off the petals and rinse the clay off with warm water. I like to follow this up with witch hazel astringent and a good face cream.

ANGELICA
Angelica archangelica

𝒳✻ Angelica is a sacred herb of Medieval Europe. ❧ It was believed to have special powers to ward off plagues and poisons. Angelica was given the folk name of the Holy Ghost Root. ❧ During World War One it was chewed for protection against the influenza epidemics. ❧

𝒳✻ Angelica is native to Europe and is a traditional plant in the European herb gardens. ❧ It was grown and used in the early colonial medicinal gardens and easily adapted itself to the wild. ❧ The colonists candied angelica, using it to decorate their cakes and pastries. ❧

𝒳✻ Herbalists have valued angelica because it is helpful to the digestive system. ❧ The stocks can be eaten raw and added to salads. ❧ The essential oil is used in the flavoring of vermouth. ❧ The oil also is used in making perfumes. ❧ It gained the name Masterwort in the old herbal books for its healing properties in strengthening the immune system. ❧

❧ Angelica is a perennial herb growing to six feet tall. ❧ The leaves are tooth leaflets which grow largest near the plant's stock. ❧ It has a thick hollow stem. Its umbrella flower head is covered with white greenish flowers. ❧ It is an aromatic herb and is sweet smelling. ❧ It grows wild in the wetlands from Minnesota to Maryland and likes rich garden soil, morning sun and afternoon shade. ❧ It can be grown by seeds in the fall, or by dividing the roots. ❧ Remember to give this giant plenty of room to move, for it will tower over the garden with its angel like protection for all the plants below. ❧

ANGELICA SYRUP

❧ This syrup can help soothe a cough or sore throat. Note that Angelica is a powerful emmenagogue and too much can bring on a woman's menses. It should not be used during pregnancy

- ❧ two cups of spring water
- ❧ one-fourth cup of angelica root finely chopped
- ❧ one-half cup of elderberries fresh or dried
- ❧ one shot glass of good brandy
- ❧ one-half cup of honey

❧ Boil the water and pour into a jar with the elderberries and angelica root and steep for 5 minutes. Strain the herbs remembering to use the back of a wooden spoon to squeeze out all the herbal juices. Put in stainless steel pan reheat and add the honey and stir. Take off the heat and add a shot of brandy to the herbal brew. Now bottle in a clean glass container and keep in the refrigerator. This syrup can be taken three teaspoons at a time for colds and coughs.

LOTUS
Nymphaea

What the rose is to the West the Lotus blossom is to the East. It is the sacred flower of Buddha, Brahma and the God Vishnu. It's Latin name *Nymphaea* contains the word nymph, the beautiful water sprite that resides in the pools of fairy tales.

The Hindus believe Brahma was bought forth from the Lotus blossom.

From the calyx of the Lotus all of creation was born. Vishnu the Preserver has a Lotus springing from his navel. Four thousand years ago the Egyptians held sacred the beans of the Lotus. The Lotus flower has been found in their architectural ornaments and decorating the tombs of their dead for the long journey to the afterlife. ❧

❧ Buddha taught the Lotus Sutra and left his teachings unfolding in the petals of enlightenment written down in this sacred text used to this day. ❧

❧ Lotus is a water plant and can be easily grown in all zones, if you stick to growing the hardier varieties. ❧ The tropical types, usually in the colors purple or blue, can be grown only in warmer climates. ❧

❧ The leaves are rounded and notched and float on top of the water while their root stock reaches down into the muddy soil below. ❧ The stalks are attached at the notch of each leaf. ❧ Flowers usually float on the surface of the water or stand on a stiff stalk above the leaf. ❧

❧ You can grow lotus in as little as eight to twelve inches of water. ❧ Use a small tub, but avoid redwood for it discolors the water. ❧ Put some rich potting soil in your tub and set the Lotus rhizome in the earth horizontally. ❧ The best time for planting is in February through October in milder climates, or April through July in cold climates. ❧

❧ Fertilize the soil with a three-to-five nitrogen product. ❧ Then add at least twelve inches of water to your tub. ❧ Keep the Lotus plants clean by picking off any dead leaves or dead flowers. ❧ The lotus blooms in warm weather and goes dormant during colder months. ❧

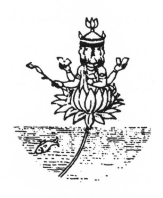

LOTUS LEAF GIFT WRAP

❧ *One birthday I was given a unique gift, a birthday present in a lotus leaf. The present itself was a satin bag but the wrapper was my favorite part. You can obtain dried lotus leaves in Chinatown. They are often used to serve rice instead of a paper plate. Buy the leaf itself and wrap birthday cards or a small present inside. Close it with a golden ribbon and you will be giving a rare and memorable gift.*

PEARLY EVERLASTING

Anaphalis margaritacea

✿ Many years ago I danced with a group of beautiful women on Mt. Shasta. ✿ We would perform for the Spring or Autumn Equinox. ✿ Everyone wore angelic white dresses splashed with colored ribbons and flowers. ✿ For one performance I wore Pearly Everlasting flowers I had found on one of my walks. ✿ I gathered them when their buds were still tight and not fully opened and took them home and tied them into a bundle and hung them upside down to dry. ✿ When they were fully dried I worked them around a metal wire shaped for my head. ✿ The result was a beautiful crown of white flowers and ribbons. ✿

✻ Pearly Everlasting grows one to three feet tall. ❧ It has narrow gray green leaves and flower heads that look like pearls before they open. ❧ As the flower opens they burst into smaller white flowers with yellow centers. ❧ Pearly Everlasting grows in poor soil, usually sand or gravel, and likes dry conditions. ❧ When collecting this plant, be sure to gather before it starts to go to seed if you are using them for dried flowers. ❧ The flowers are aromatic and native to many states in North America. ❧

✻ They are also known as Lady's Tobacco, for they are used in a mild smoking mixture, usually mixed with coltsfoot and mullein. ❧ The pioneers used them for pillow stuffing. ❧ Herbalists use this plant as an astringent and expectorant. ❧ Pearly Everlasting gained its name from the lasting ability the flowers have when dried. ❧

HERBAL SMOKING MIXTURE

❧ *This mixture is helpful for those who would like to quit the tobacco habit. When the urge to smoke is overwhelming these calming herbs will give a measure of relief. Mix one cup of coltsfoot, one cup of raspberry leaf, one-eighth cup of pearly everlasting flowers and twenty dried mullein flowers. Use dried herbs, mix together and store in a sealed container. This mixture can comfort those who are breaking the smoking habit. Roll the herbal mixture in a cigarette paper and smoke only when the urge is overwhelming. It is better not to settle for half-way measures.*

FLOWER POWER is available to all of us equally. ❧ A pretty face or great wealth is not required to bring flowers into your daily life, whether for their healing properties, ceremonies, eating, wearing their fragrance, bathing, arranging, as well as growing. ❧

❧ Flowers can change your outlook, no matter how difficult your circumstances. ❧ Those who are unable to grow their own, or to purchase commercially grown plants or cuttings almost certainly have access to public parks and gardens where you can surround yourself with beauty and fragrance. ❧ An hour spent in such an environment is quality time, private and peaceful. ❧

When you encounter any of the twenty-two "wisdom flowers" you've just been reading about, you might meditate on the meaning that wisdom has for you. And consider the cycles each flower experiences. Everything has its season. What goes around comes around. If this be the winter of your discontent, can Spring be far behind?

Doing this book certainly has made my life bloom anew. It is my hope some of these pages will do the same for you.

ABOUT THE AUTHOR

IF ever there was a quintessential "Flower Child." Raylene Veltri must have been it. ❧ Friends say she has the face of a flower; certainly one that appears happiest when buried in blossoms. ❧ ❧ Raylene grew up digging in Mother Earth and has remained a student of Nature's teachings ever since. ❧ Raylene and her husband, John, a photojournalist specializing in Native American cultures, have worked as a team recording the lore and memorabilia of numerous Indian Tribes. ❧

❧ An herbalist by training and vocation, Mrs. Veltri's plant knowledge is put to use teaching, guiding nature walks and conducting workshops both East and West. ❧ While preferring the outdoor venue, she has appeared in numerous herbal, health, and healing TV shows and videos. ❧

❧ *A Woman's Garden of Wisdom* is not Raylene's first or last work. ❧ She has written *Nature Knows Best, Wildcrafting in Woodstock, Flowers of the Heart,* and *Gardening in a Pot.* ❧ Halo Books will soon publish another of her titles, *The Garden Speaks.* ❧

❧ When she isn't writing, walking, lecturing, and hosting, Mrs. Veltri is the mother to three children Joshua, Sheenon and Selene. ❧ The Veltri's home is Fairfax, California. ❧

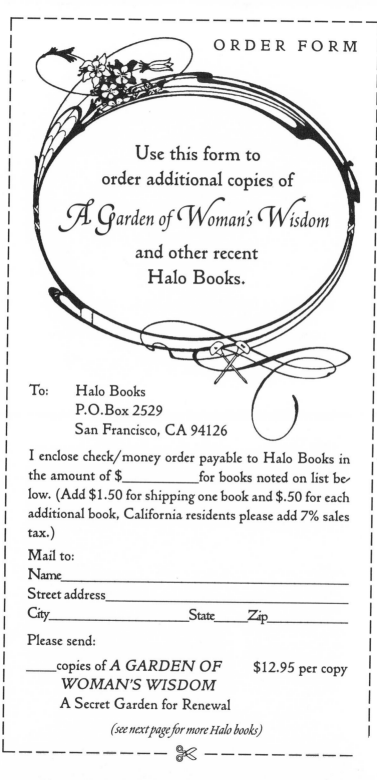

ORDER FORM

Use this form to
order additional copies of

A Garden of Woman's Wisdom

and other recent
Halo Books.

To: Halo Books
      P.O. Box 2529
      San Francisco, CA 94126

I enclose check/money order payable to Halo Books in
the amount of $_____ for books noted on list be-
low. (Add $1.50 for shipping one book and $.50 for each
additional book, California residents please add 7% sales
tax.)

Mail to:
Name_____
Street address_____
City_____State____Zip_____

Please send:

____copies of *A GARDEN OF* $12.95 per copy
      WOMAN'S WISDOM
      A Secret Garden for Renewal

(see next page for more Halo books)

____copies of *TIME HAPPENS* $13.95 per copy
   You Could Not Have Picked a Better Time To
   Be Fiftysomething

____copies of *SUDDENLY SINGLE!* $13.95 per copy
   A Lifeline For Anyone Who Has Lost A Love

____copies of *IF HE LOVES ME* $12.95 per copy
   WHY DOESN'T HE TELL ME?

____copies of *TEENAGE* $11.95 per copy
   SURVIVAL MANUAL
   Being in charge of your own
   mind and body.

____copies of *AM I A HINDU?* $14.95 per copy
   The Hinduism Primer.

____copies of *YOUR SEXUAL HEALTH* $15.95 per copy
   What teenagers need to know about sexually
   transmitted diseases and pregnancy.

____copies of *YOU ARE MY FRIEND* $9.95 per copy
   A celebration of friendship.

____copies of *LOVING CHILDREN* $9.95 per copy
   Words of love about kids
   from those who cherish them.

✱ For a free catalog of all Halo Books in print, write address above.

✱ Retailers should order from their wholesaler or Halo's national distributor, Atrium Publishing Group, 3356 Coffey Lane, Santa Rosa, CA 95403. Telephone 1-800-275-2606.

Thank you.   71 569IDA 79L0
                   FS
            12/95 30910-173

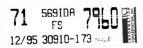